Super Fun
Brain Challenges

The Invisible Ghost

Hold the book about 16 inches from your eyes.
Look at the mouth of the ghost for 30 seconds.
What do you see at the castle's entrance?

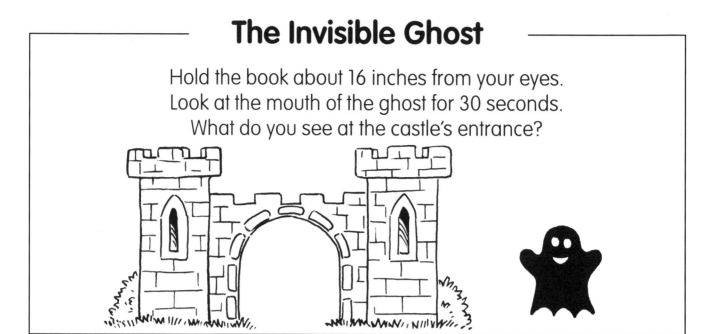

Pairs

Nelson

Amber

Which objects belong together in pairs?

Connect the Numbers

Connect all the numbers that are divisible by three,
from small to large, and see what frightens the small cat.

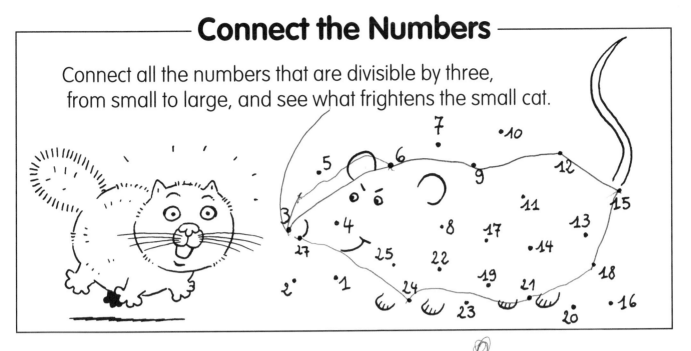

Tomato Humor

Hello, I know a great joke!
But I'll tell it in tomato language!

WTOHTOATOTTO ITOSTO GTORTOETOETONTO
ATONTODTO STOPTOITONTOSTO
ATORTOOTOUTONTODTO?

STOPTOITONTOATOCTOHTO!

Do you understand what I'm saying?

Handwritten annotations: WHAT IS GREEN / AND SPINS / AROUND? / SPINACH

Mr. Bear's Machine

Turn the first gear in the direction of the black arrow.
What direction will the last gear turn?
Color the correct arrow.

Magic Square

The horizontal, vertical, and diagonal sums are all 15.
Can you figure out the missing numbers?

	9	2	→ 15
3			→ 15
		1	→ 15

→ 15

Catherine the Cowgirl

Look at the negatives and find these two photos from Catherine's costume party.

A.

5

B.

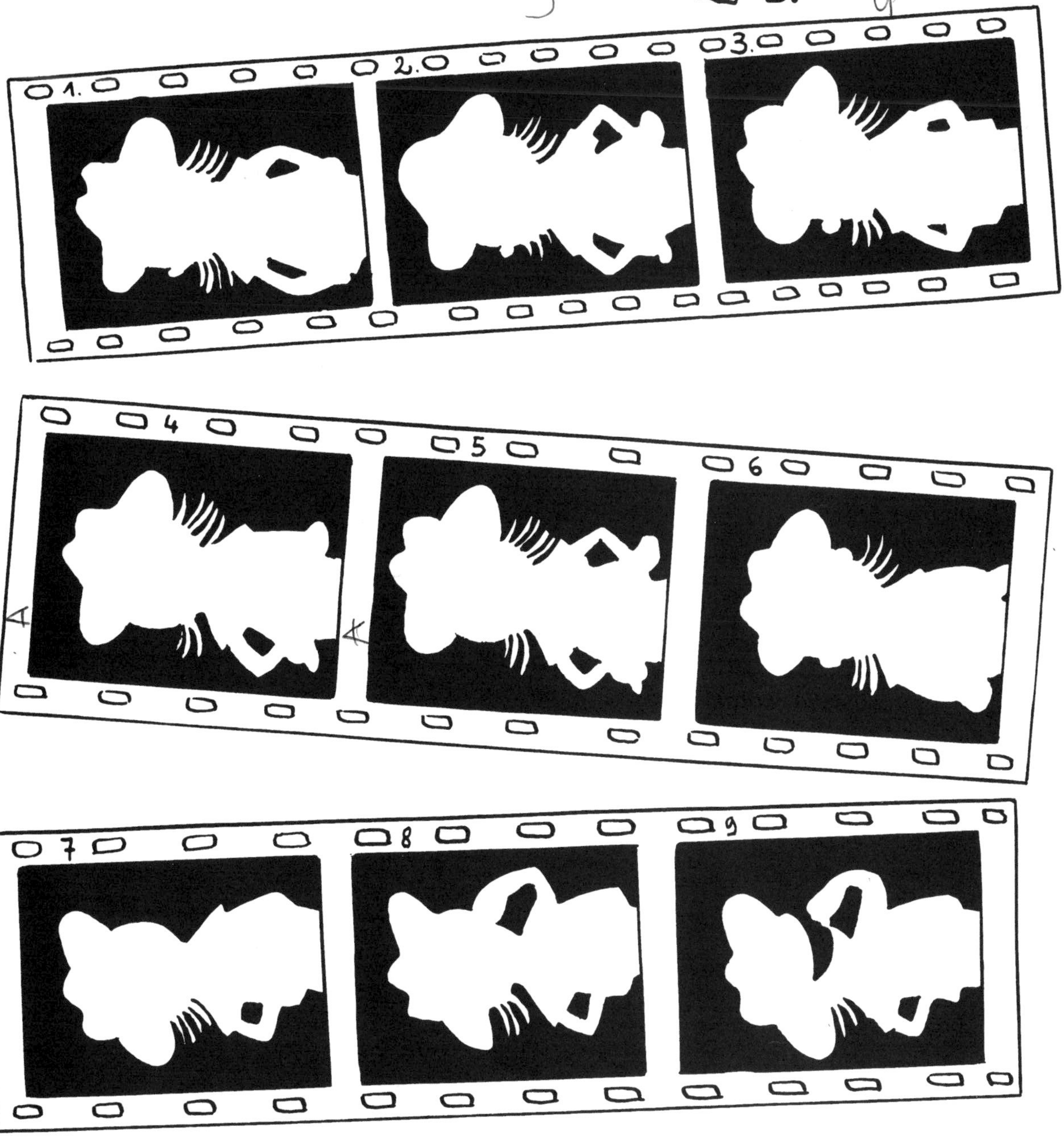

9

1.

2.

3.

4.

5.

6.

7.

8.

9.

On the Scale

How much does each animal weigh?
Fill in the correct weight below.

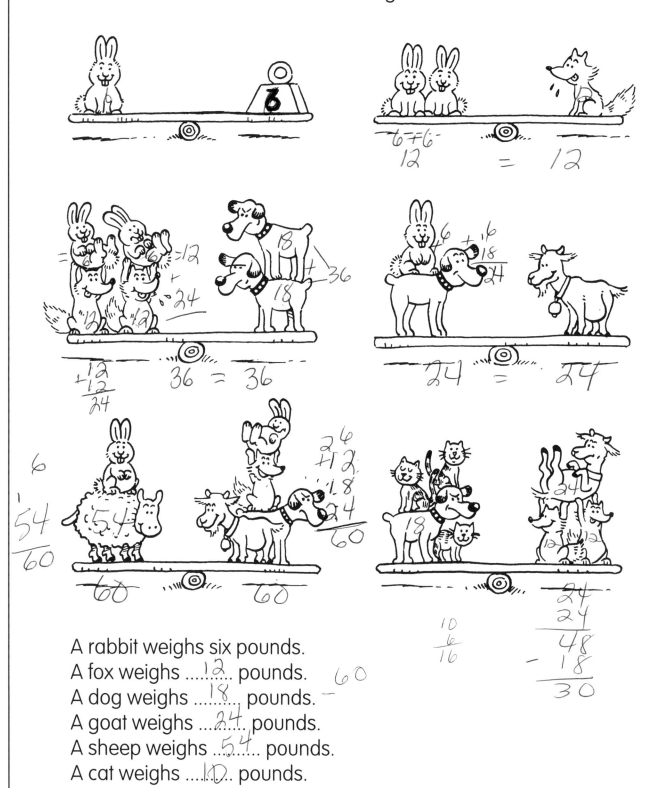

A rabbit weighs six pounds.
A fox weighs ....12.... pounds.
A dog weighs ....18.... pounds.
A goat weighs ...24.... pounds.
A sheep weighs ...54.... pounds.
A cat weighs ....10.. pounds.

Morse Code

Below is the alphabet in Morse code. However, some Morse codes are missing. You'll find the missing codes if you first decode the two sayings on the cards below.

A .—	H	O ———	V
B —...	I ..	P .——.	W .——
C —.—.	J .———	Q ——.—	X —..—
D —..	K	R .—.	Y —.——
E .	L .—..	S ...	Z ——..
F	M ——	T —	
G	N —.	U	

1.
———/..—/—// ———/.—./..//...//.//——./....//—//

———/..—/—// ———/..—.//——/../—./—..//

2.
.——/....//.—/—.//—/....//.//—.—./.—/—//../...//.—/—.—./.—/——//

—/....//——/../—./——.//—./../—./...//.—/../.—./.——/—./...//

Dominoes

The dominoes are in the correct order, but they need to be turned so that you can read a word on the top and bottom.

What Day Is It?

Joey has drawing lessons on Wednesday and Saturday.
On Tuesday and Thursday, he goes to music school.
He plays basketball every Tuesday, Wednesday, and Saturday.
On Friday and Saturday, he has a Judo lesson.
Today, Joey drew and played basketball.
He also went to his Judo lesson,
but he didn't go to music school.
What is the day today?

Drawing Animals

Finish these four drawings.
The words under the drawings indicate what each should be.

a pig   **a monkey**   **a cat**   **a bear**

Pig Hunt

The wolf runs 100 yards in 25 seconds.
Pig 1 runs 200 yards in 30 seconds.
Pig 2 runs 50 yards in 5 seconds.
Pig 3 runs 400 yards in 80 seconds.

Can the wolf
catch a pig?
Who runs the
fastest?

Pirate Game

Find nine boats in the grid.
* The boats cannot touch one another, not even diagonally.
* The numbers indicate how many boats are in the surrounding squares.
* No boats can be in the boxes containing flags.
Hint: Cross out the boxes that cannot contain boats.

Adding Fruit

Can you help the monkeys find the sum?
Every piece of fruit equals a number.
Try to find the numbers based on the information given.

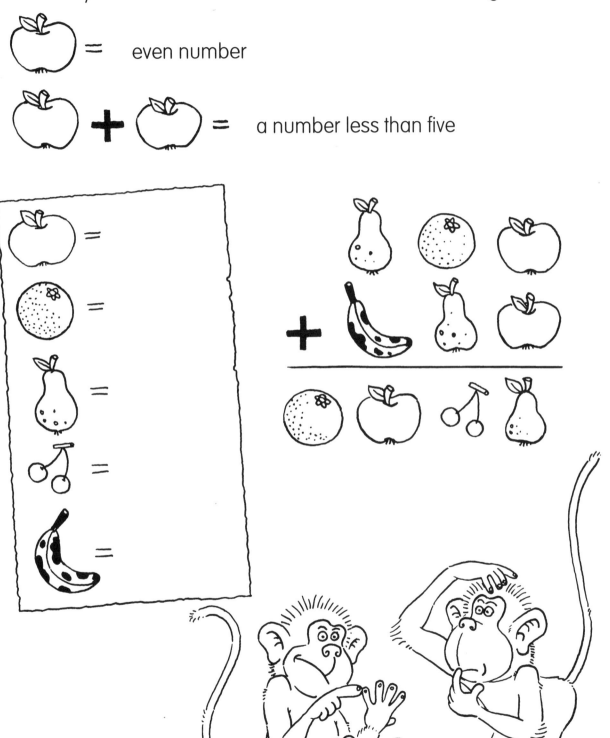

Magic Fork

How many teeth does this fork have?

Star Gazer

The second circle contains one more star. Find and color it.

Age

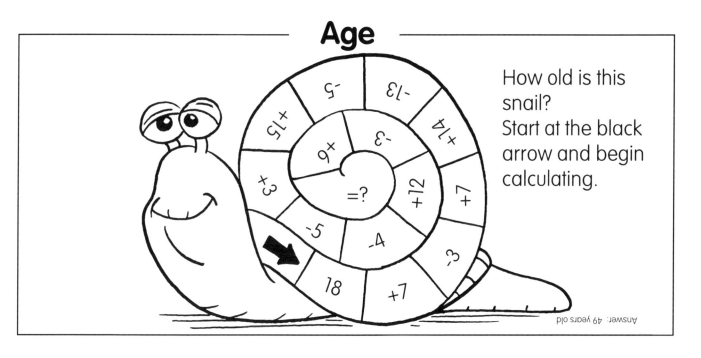

How old is this snail?
Start at the black arrow and begin calculating.

Dinospots

Find the three spots that are missing from the dinosaur's back and color them.

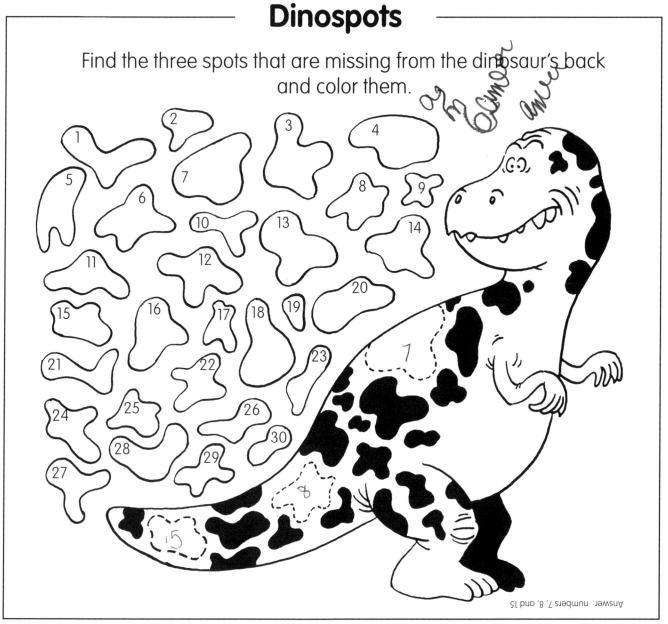

Hungry Worms

The grid contains six apples. A worm is ready to eat an apple.
The worm is seven squares long. Draw another five worms that are seven
squares long. Each worm must be ready to eat an apple.

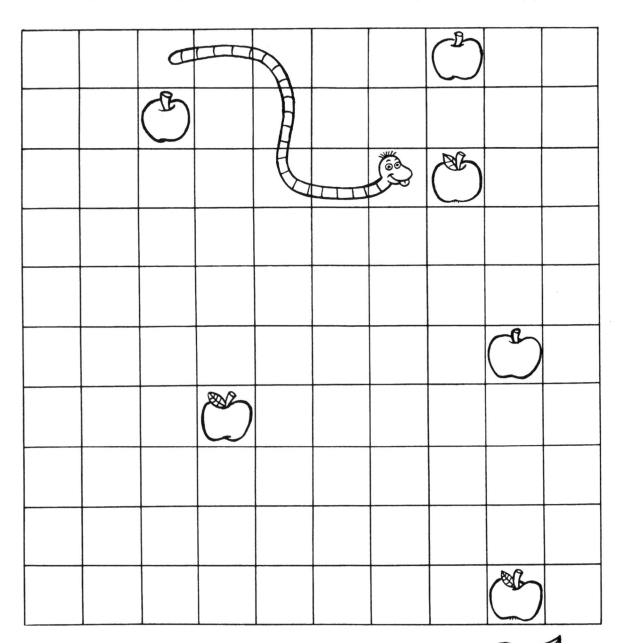

Be careful!
The squares with a worm must not
touch one another, not even the
corners.

Letter Monsters

The monsters have eaten some letters from the texts.
Use the letters on each monster's t-shirt to complete the texts again.

NIGHT
TABLE
PI • • O
BE • CH
C • RDBO • RD

B • D
• U • HOR
DE • • IS •
R • I • BOW

NAT

CIGA •
WA • P
LIVING-
• OOM

• L • CTRIC
• • L
• • • P • CT
CH • CK

RES

Rosettes

Which of the two circles in the middle of the rosettes is the largest?

A.

B.

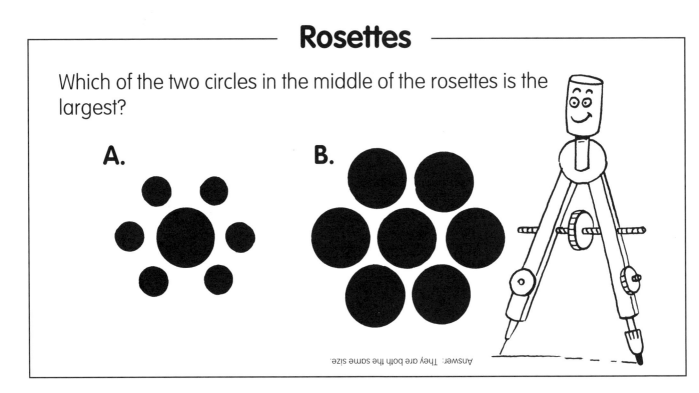

Answer: They are both the same size.

In the Moonlight

Color the shapes containing crosses. What do you see?

Squirrel

How many black squares are completely hidden behind the squirrel?

Cubes

A corner block is missing from the small cube.

How many blocks are missing from the large cube?

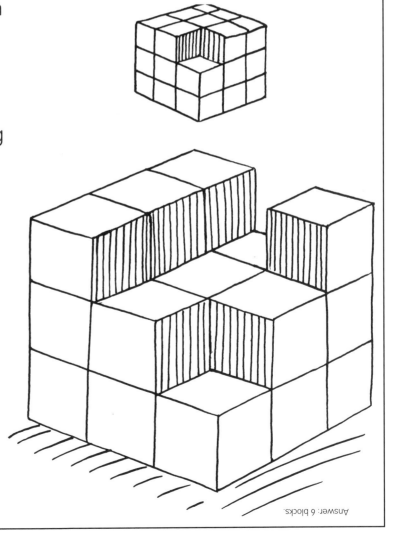

Animal Kingdom Intruders

Find the animal in each group that does not belong there.
Do you know why that animal doesn't belong in the group?

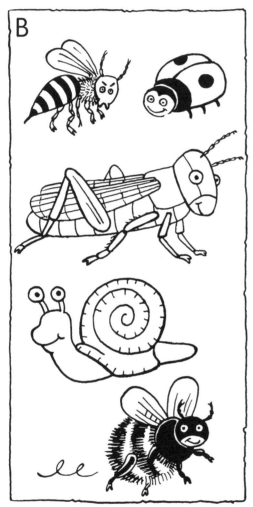

Favorite Animal

Find the picture that doesn't belong in each row and write that word on the dotted line. Do the same for each row.

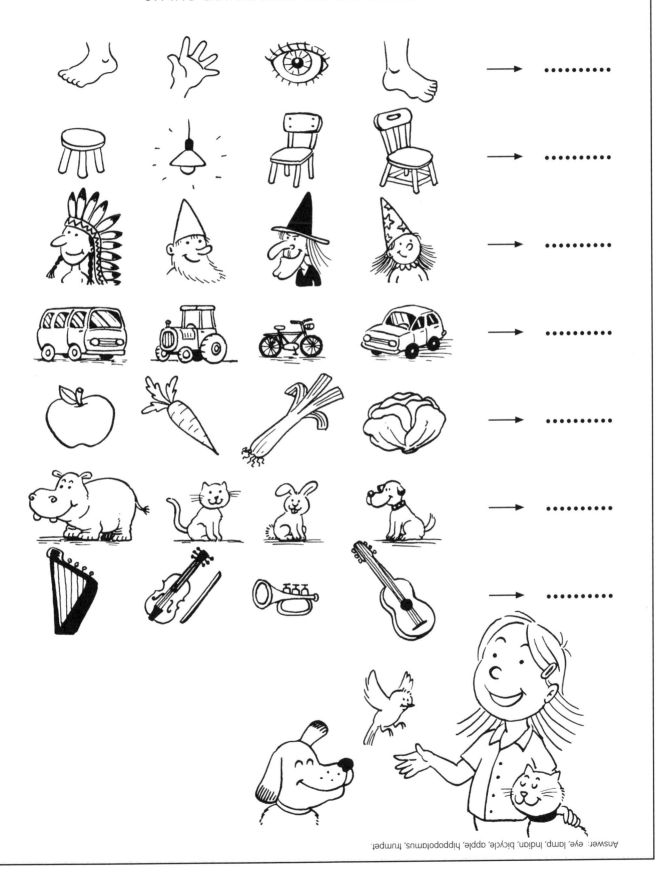

Flying Saucers

Almost all these UFO's are a little different from one another.
Find the three flying saucers that are exactly the same.

Grandma's Hat

Sophie has put Grandma's hat on her head. Find the picture with the same hat as the one that Sophie has on her head

Logical Series

Find the missing letter at the end of each row.

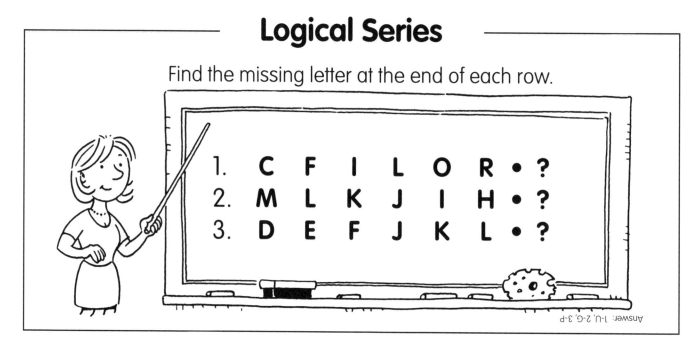

1. C   F   I   L   O   R • ?
2. M   L   K   J   I   H • ?
3. D   E   F   J   K   L • ?

The Correct Order

The pictures are mixed up. What is the correct order?

The correct order is: ....

Line Segments

Which of the two line segments is the longest?

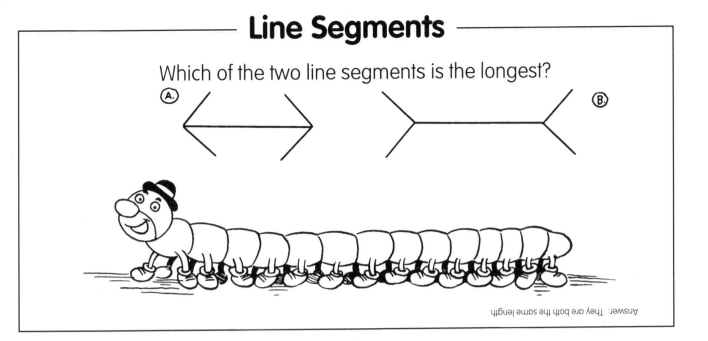

A.

B.

Straight or Curved

Are the lines of the square straight or curved?

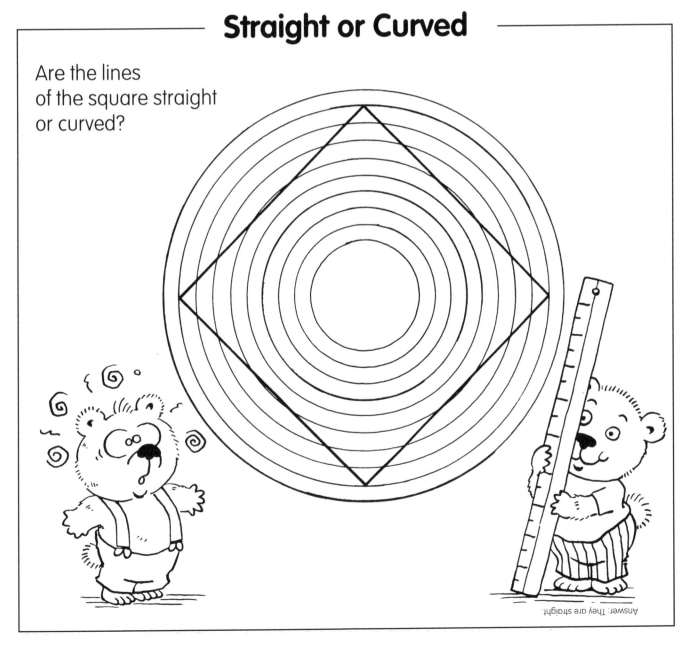

Calculation Blocks

Fill in the missing numbers and operations.

	:		=	
+	■	x	■	
8	-		=	3
=	■	=	■	=
	-	10	=	8

51	+		=	61
	■		■	
31	-	1	=	
=	■	=	■	=
	+		=	31

The sums on both sides of the equal signs must all be the same.
Example: 3 x 2 = 5 + 1 = 6

6		12	=	21	-	3	=	
+	■		■	+	■	+	■	+
	+	16	=			5	=	26
=	■	=	■	=	■	=	■	=
16	+		=	52	-			=	

	-	5	=	83	-		=	6
+	■	x	■		■		■	
19	:	1	=		+	2	=	
=	■	=	■	=	■	=	■	=
	-		=		-	75	=	

The Number Monster

The number monster has filled his stomach.
However, he didn't find several numbers tasty, so he didn't eat them. Do you know why? The numbers that the number monster didn't like are not divisible by ...... or ..... but by ....

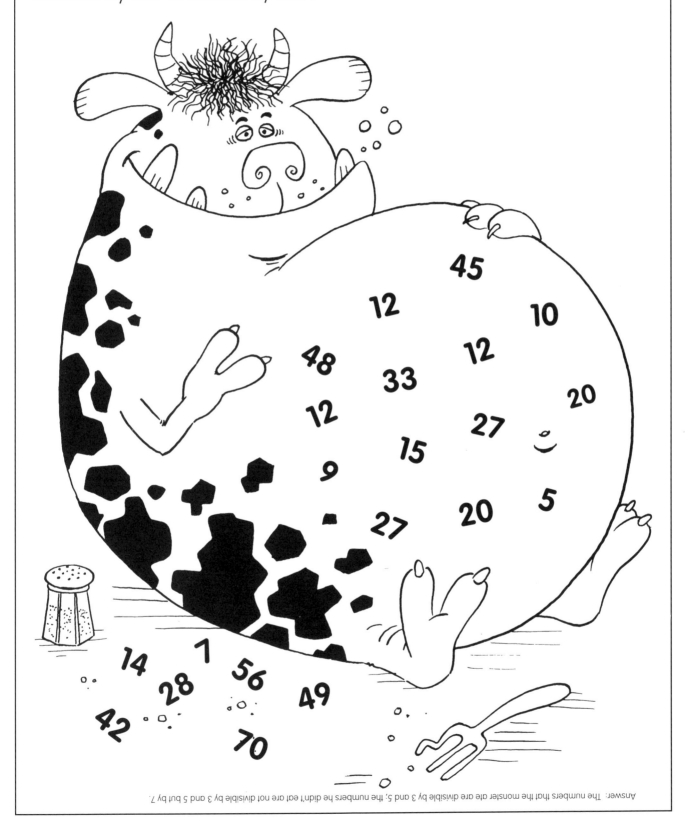

Riddles

1. What has eyes on all sides but still can't see?

2. What can fall through a window without breaking the glass?

3. When you see more of it, you see less of it ...

4. If you speak, it no longer exists...

Answer: 1. dice 2. light 3. dusk 4. silence

The Invisible Tiger

A tiger is hidden in this grid.
Color the squares according to the coordinates below
and see the tiger appear.

COLOR THESE SQUARES ORANGE:
E7-E9-E10-E11-E12-E14-E15-E16 / F6-F9-F10-F11-F12-F13-F17- / G4-G5-G10-G11-G12-G13-G14-G18 / H3-H4-H11-H12-H13-H18-H19 / I2-I3-I10-I11-I12-I13-I14-I19 / J3-J9-J10-J11-J12-J13-J14-J15-J20 / K1-K8-K9-K15-K16-K20-K21 / L8-L9-L10-L14-L15-L16-L17-L20 / M8-M16-M17 / N17 / O17 / P16-P17 / Q16 / S1 / T1-T21 / U1-U2-U20-U21

COLOR THESE SQUARES BROWN:
B4-B5-B17-B18 / C3-C6-C16-C19 / D2-D7-D15-D20 / E2-E20 / F3-F18-F19 / I5-I6-I17-I18 / J6-J7-J8-J16-J17 / K7-K17 / L7 / M6-M7 / N7 / O6-O7 / P7 / Q1-Q7-Q8 / R1-R9-R15-R21 / S2-S9-S15-S21 / T2-T3-T9-T10-T14-T20 / U3-U4-U8-U9-U10-U11-U13-U14-U15-U19

COLOR THESE SQUARES GREEN:
H7-H15

COLOR THESE SQUARES PINK:
K11-K12-K13 / L12 / M12

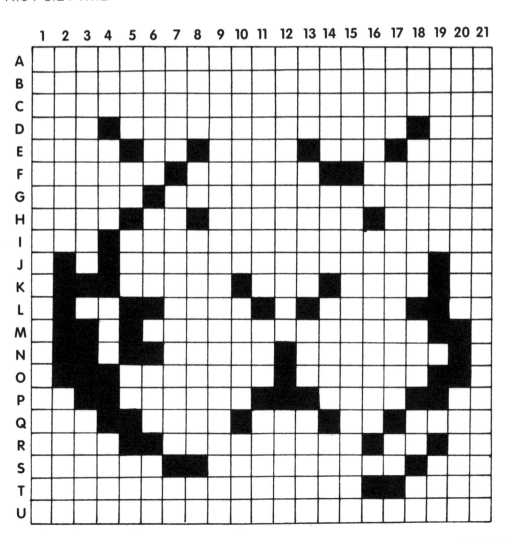

Cubes

Which cube is the mouse folding up?

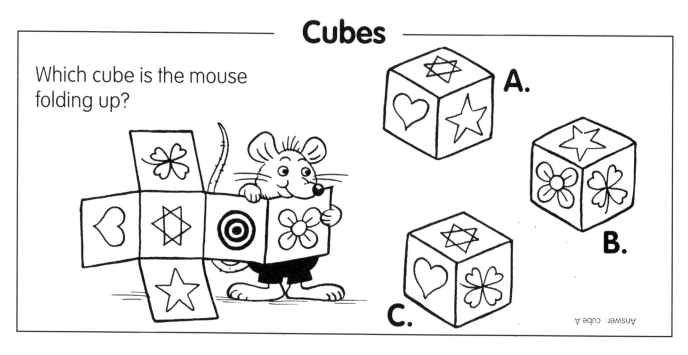

A.

B.

C.

Hidden Hearts

How many boxes with hearts are hidden behind the elephant?

Butterflies

How many butterflies are there?

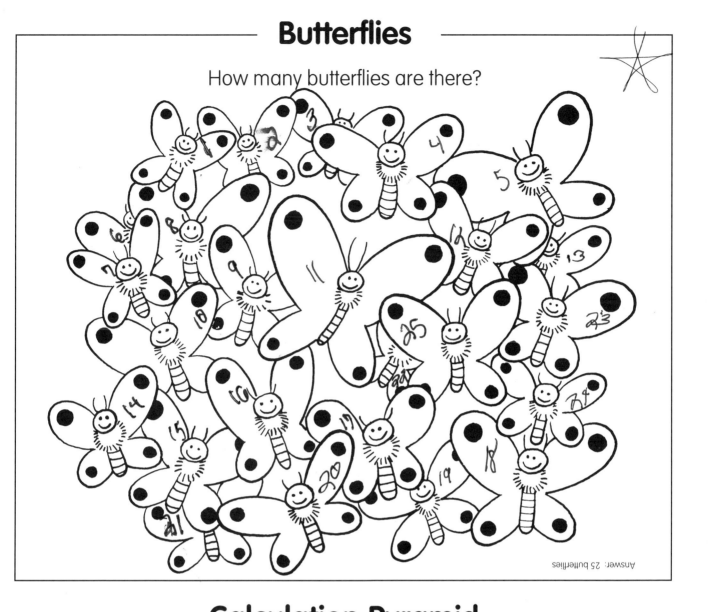

Calculation Pyramid

Every stone in the pyramid must have a number that equals the sum of the two stones below it. Can you figure out what the missing stones are?

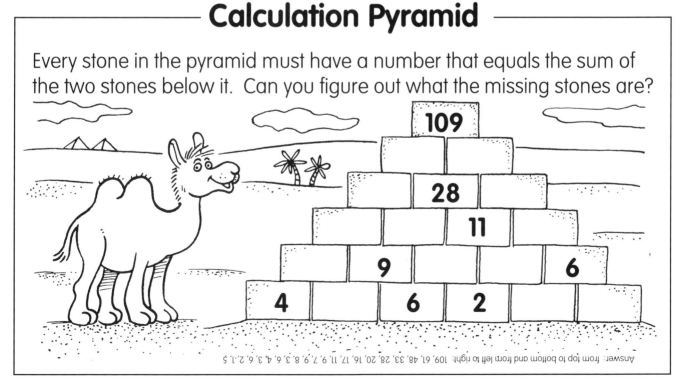

		109		
		28		
			11	
	9			6
4		6	2	

Making Faces

Find the correct mirror image for each monster!

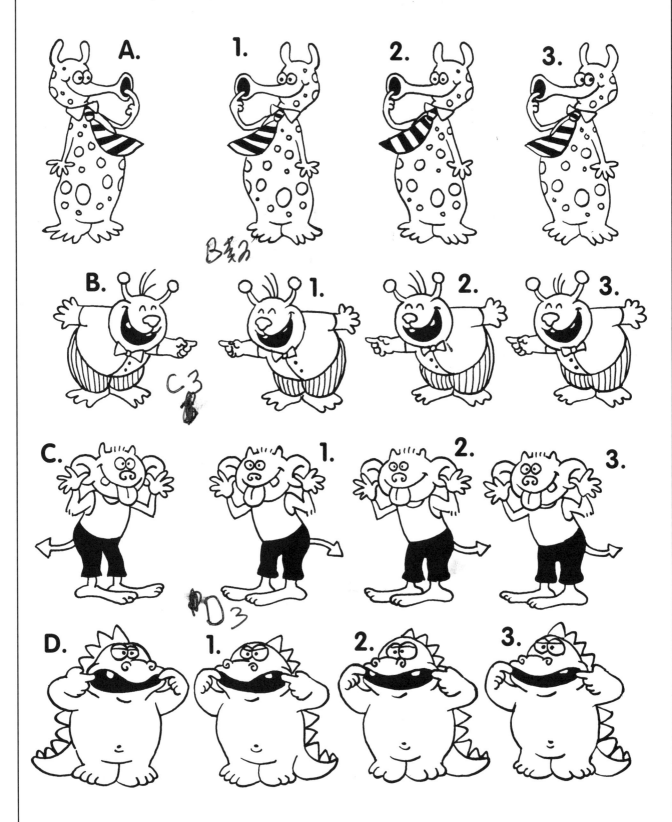

Bear Band

Can you find ten differences between the two pictures?.

Chicks

Two chicks belonging to Carmela are running between the chicks belonging to Betty. Carmela's chicks have a number that is not divisible by 4. Color these chicks.

Grid Search

Find these squares in the grid:

Color this square green.

Color this square red.

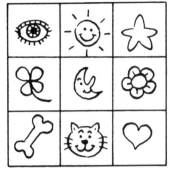

Color this square yellow.

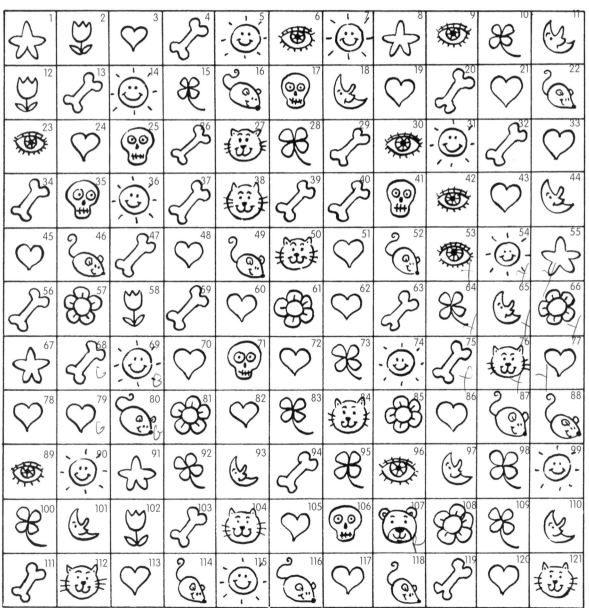

Blocks

Place the blocks in the grid.
Three blocks have already been placed to help you.

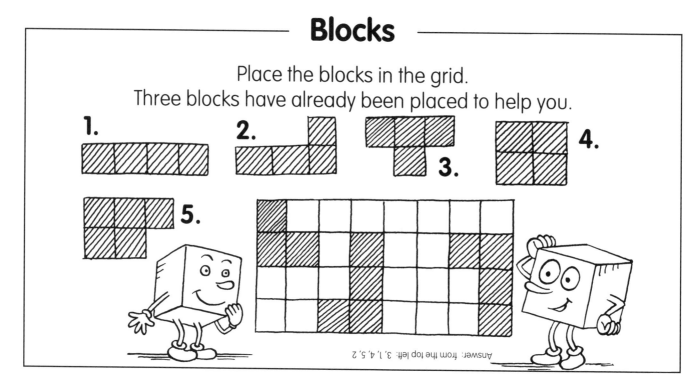

1. **2.** **3.** **4.**

5.

Word Search

What word is hidden in this grid?
The boxes with a smiley face indicate the place of that letter in the word.

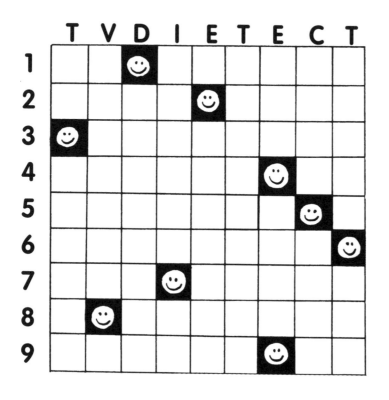

T V D I E T E C T

1
2
3
4
5
6
7
8
9

Blackboard

Which number is missing from this board?

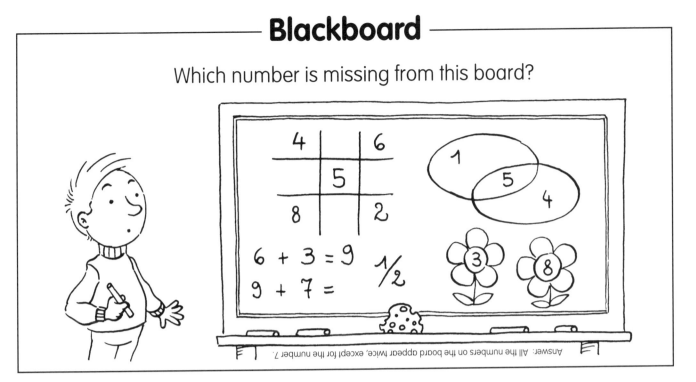

"The Curled Tail" Restaurant

The wind has blown away all the words from the menu board.
Recreate the menu using the words on the ground.

Menu of the Day

Appetizer:
....

Main Course:
....

Dessert:
....

ASP   AP   PIE   ESE   LED   SOUP   CHE
GRILL   ARA   PLE   GUS

Count the Objects

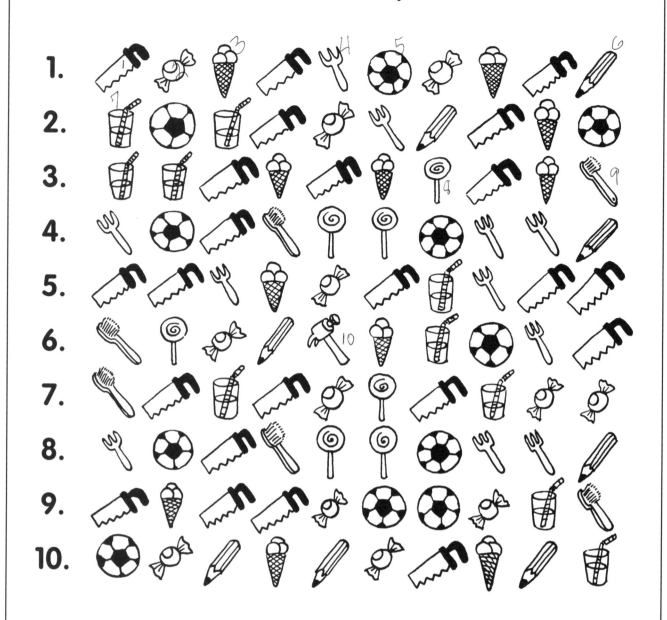

1. How many different objects do you see? ....

2. Which object appears only once? ....

3. Which object appears the most? ....

4. Is there a row in which all the objects appear? ....

Treasure Chest

How much is each item in the grid worth? Find five numbers.
The total sum of the objects of each row appears at the end of each row.
Hint: The total sum of the five rings in the fourth row is ten.
How much is each ring worth?

ring	diamond	diamond	necklace	coin	**16**
ring	crown	necklace	crown	necklace	**16**
necklace	coin	diamond	necklace	crown	**16**
ring	ring	ring	ring	ring	**10**
ring	diamond	ring	coin	diamond	**15**
11	**17**	**17**	**13**	**15**	

◯ = ... ◯ = ... 👑 = ... ◎ = ... ◇ = ...

Heavy, Heavier, Heaviest

Which dog weighs the most?

The heaviest dog weighs as much as the pig.
Draw the second heaviest dog on the seesaw.

Hoisting Crane

Which way should Mrs. Bear
turn the handle to lift the load?
Color the correct arrow.

Stick Riddle

Of course, 1-3 does not equal 2!

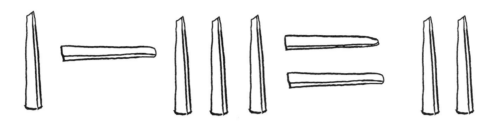

Move one stick to make the problem correct.

Answer: Place the bottom stick of the equal sign under the minus sign; then you'll have 1=3-2.

Snail Race

A snail has to climb over a wall.
The wall is 60 feet high.
Each day the snail climbs 15 feet, but each night it slides down 12 feet.
How many days will it take for the snail reaches the top of the wall?

Answer: The snail will reach the top of the wall on day 16.

Dividing Up Treats

50 treats are divided among five children
- Thomas gets 13 treats.
- Tim gets twice as many treats as Jan.
- Jan gets as many treats as Larry.
- Lisa gets 10 treats fewer than Thomas.
- Jan gets 5 treats more than Lisa.

How many treats are left over?

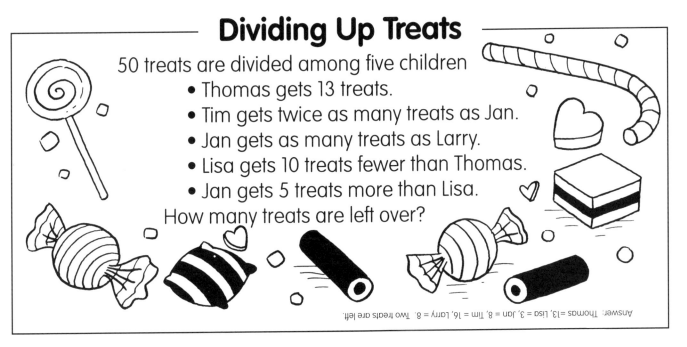

Answer: Thomas =13, Lisa = 3, Jan = 8, Tim = 16, Larry = 8. Two treats are left.

Word Wall

Cross out all words containing the letter "r" or "ll."
Cross out all words that begin with "s."
What is the sentence you read from top to bottom?

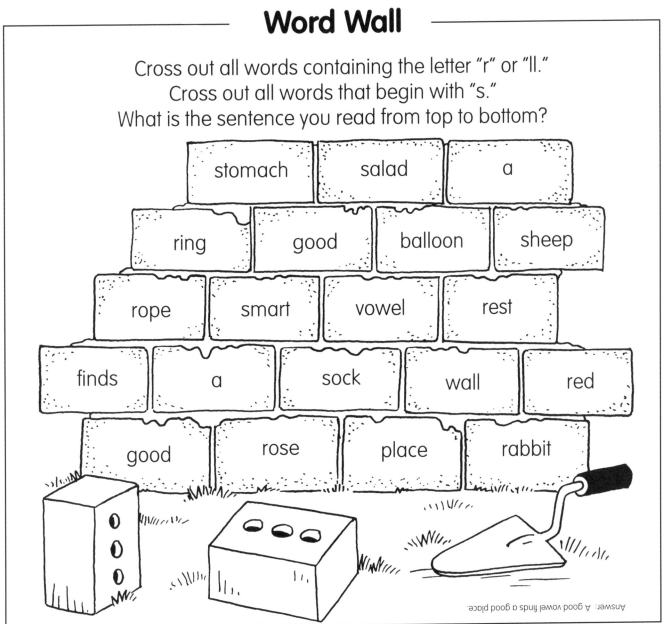

stomach	salad	a
ring	good	balloon	sheep
rope	smart	vowel	rest
finds	a	sock	wall	red
good	rose	place	rabbit

Answer: A good vowel finds a good place.

Check Out Counter

Add all the numbers up and write the total that Mrs. Mouse has to pay.

Weight Lifting

How many pounds is Willy
the gorilla lifting?
Solve the problem on the sign.

$$(35 + 23 + 7 + 14 + 3 + 12 + 6) \times 2$$

Quiz Master Owl

Do you know the answers to all of Mr. Owl's quiz questions?
How many points have you scored?

2. What is the capital of Italy?
5 points

1. Who was Mozart?
20 points

3. Who was the first man on the moon?
10 points

4. Who discovered America?
10 points

5. What is the boiling point of water?
5 points

6. Who painted the Mona Lisa?
20 points

7. Who was Picasso?
20 points

8. What is the difference between an Asian camel and an African camel?
2 points

9. How long does it take for the earth to circle the sun?
5 points

Answer: 1. a composer 2. Rome 3. Armstrong 4. Columbus 5. 212 degrees Fahrenheit 6. Da Vinci 7. a painter 8. An Asian camel has two humps, an African camel has one hump. 9. 365 days

Block Towers

The mice have built a block tower.
How many blocks did they use to build it?

How many blocks are still
in the wagon?

Agent 007 has received a message, but it's written in code. Can you break the code?

W T A H C T
U O Y A U O R B E
G E I N F W O
O L D E L

Answer: Watch out! You're being followed.

Scarecrows

Find the ten differences between the two drawings.

Answer: 1. The tail of the mouse in the hat. 2. Bangs on the scarecrow. 3. Tail on bird. 4. The seam on the scarecrow's jaw. 5. The shading on the patch on the coat front. 6. Extra button. 7. Extra finger on glove. 8. Shading on knee patch. 9. Extra shoelace. 10. Bird's eyes closed.

Strange Symbols

Which symbol should follow in this row and why?

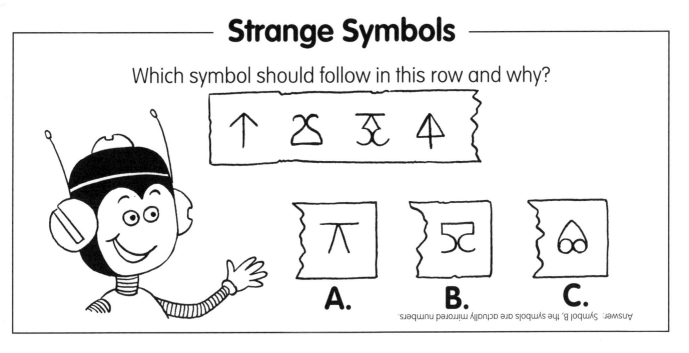

A. **B.** **C.**

Deep Thinkers

In which chest will Pirate Paul find the treasure?

There's nothing in this chest.

Only one of these chests is right choice.

Pirate's Treasure

Help Pirate Paul find the key to open the treasure chest.
Make sure that the sum of all the numbers in each row equals 100.
The bold number in the box indicates the correct key.
Which is the correct key?